Journey to Prague a[nd]
Barrie

Journey to Prague and other Mileage

Barrie David

Published by Barrie David, 2023.

While every precaution has been taken in the preparation of this book, the publisher assumes no responsibility for errors or omissions, or for damages resulting from the use of the information contained herein.

JOURNEY TO PRAGUE AND OTHER MILEAGE

First edition. November 12, 2023.

Copyright © 2023 Barrie David.

ISBN: 979-8223364801

Written by Barrie David.

Also by Barrie David

Memories of Mileage Past
Journey to Prague and other Mileage

Table of Contents

CHAPTER ONE 1
CHAPTER TWO 6
CHAPTER THREE 13
CHAPTER FOUR 21
CHAPTER FIVE 25
CHAPTER SIX 34
CHAPTER SEVEN 38
CHAPTER EIGHT 53

To my wife Elly best friend and among other things, a very supportive editor...

CHAPTER ONE

JOURNEY TO PRAGUE AND OTHER MILEAGE...

RIVER CRUISE JOURNEY

Many years ago, on a black-tie evening aboard a cruise liner, my wife Elly and I were sat at a dining table making small talk with other people when a middle-aged lady introduced herself saying her name was Mary and casually enquired if any of us had seen '*Operation Daybreak*' a Movie about the assassination of Reinhard Heydrich in Prague in June 1942. Known as the 'Butcher of Prague' and described by Hitler as "the man with the iron heart", Heydrich supervised Nazi death squads that killed millions of people. By now holding everyone's attention, Mary added the assassination was undertaken by two Czech agents trained and parachuted into Prague by the British SOE – (Special Operations Executive). Although the assassination was partially successful due to a jammed Sten gun, Heydrich later died from wounds incurred when a grenade was thrown into his open car. The two agents, Josef Gabcik and Jan Kubis, (who both served in the French Foreign Legion before being released to fight for their own country), were hiding in a Church with other agents sent to Prague by the British to assist the Czech resistance. All agents, and members of the resistance, were then betrayed by one of their own, Karel Corda.

With German troops surrounding the Church there began a fierce firefight and although Hitler issued strict orders to capture all agents alive none survived the firefight. Discovering agents were hiding in the crypt the Germans attempted to make them surrender by pushing fire brigade hoses through a street window leading to it. Aware as the crypt flooded they would face horrendous torture if captured, according to the Movie both agents committed suicide. After the war Karel Corda was executed for treason by the Czech Government. As if the story wasn't riveting enough Mary commented such was her fascination with it she went to Prague and located the Church describing in detail how the stonework around the street window used to flood the crypt still bore the scars of surrounding bullet holes. The 1975 Movie, although questioned for historical and military accuracy, was well received as a credible version of the assassination. The actual name for the assassination was '*Operation Anthropoid*'. Several more definitive Movies were to follow.

In 2019, to celebrate my 74th birthday, Elly and I went on a twelve-day river cruise up the Danube where sightseeing stops in Budapest, Bratislava, Austria and Germany where the cruise ended, the journey continued by coach to Prague where rather than flying home with the other passengers we booked into a hotel for three days primarily to locate and visit the Church Mary described, amazingly the first Prague citizen we told what we were looking for spoke excellent English and advised we were looking for Saint Cyril's Church in Resslova Street, a five-minute taxi ride away. The Church is massive and dominates the entire street, it's Crypt, apparently used in making the Movie '*Operation Daybreak*' is now a small museum, the entrance is a short walk from the bullet scarred window Mary mentioned, directly above it are two stone figures, one is a priest the other a soldier wearing a helmet and a parachute harness, beneath him are British airborne forces parachute wings. To the people of Prague the agents who died are to this day referred to as Paratroopers. The museum is small, gloomy, and tangibly atmospheric, every available wall space and square roof supporting pillars show graphic pictures recounting the assassination and the bloody aftermath when Hitler ordered savage revenge for the killing of a man he deemed to be his successor in towns such as Lidice where the entire population were slaughtered and the town itself expunged from the map.

A large heavy wooden door that opens at the slightest touch leads from the museum to the crypt where head and shoulder statues of all the agents killed are on show. On the day we visited classes of Czech school children were being educated on their country's history by their teachers. This haunting journey, inspired years earlier by a casual comment on a cruise liner, concluded when I placed the book I wanted to purchase on a counter in front of the museum's curator who smiled, gestured toward the airborne tie I was wearing. Slowly shaking his head and adamantly refusing payment he then extended his hand.

Two streets at the site of the assassination have since been named Gabcikova (Gabcik Street) and Kubisova (Kubis Street) in honour of two incredibly brave men.

Lesson learning unforgettable mileage…

CHAPTER TWO

THE FIRST PARACHUTE DESCENT

July 1972

In British airborne forces, when you prove yourself by passing a mercilessly gruelling selection course called P Company, you're ready for parachute training which ends when your presented with one of the most respected and coveted military insignia in the world. Blue and white parachute wings. When training begins, you meet men from other units, mostly Royal Marine Commandos, SAS troopers, you then meet RAF parachute instructors, smiling affable men who get the best out of you simply by raising both eyebrows. Being members of the world-famous RAF freefall team, the Falcons, it's a like having piano lessons from a concert pianist. The first three days are gobbled up inside a huge hanger where you're unrelentingly taught basic parachute landing rolls until it becomes second nature, how to exit an aircraft via a mock fuselage of a C130 Hercules, how to steer away from possible mid-air entanglements.

You advance to training aids where you step out from a thirty-five feet high platform wearing a parachute harness connected to a large propeller that slows down your descent to practice landing. Next comes an eighty-foot-high tower which is outside the main hangar. For this you ascend in a long queue up an inner stairway until it's your turn to jump in a controlled descent back to earth - it teaches additional flight safety. The 'knacker cracker' again outside, is a sort of hut on stilts about twenty feet high which simulates the buffeting on an actual exit from an aircraft - so called because great care must be taken that you keep your wedding gear well clear of the harness webbing straps either side of your groin thereby avoiding a voice three octaves higher. The endless training all lead to your first parachute descent via the fearsome barrage balloon. Boarding single decker buses driven by WAAF's, with each man carrying a steel helmet with his name on it the journey to a nearby drop zone is subdued and tensely atmospheric. On arrival every pair of eyes are drawn to two massive grey barrage balloons in the distance. A tea wagon is parked very sensibly near some toilets, and you're invited to help ourselves to both. Close by are RAF trucks carrying hundreds of parachutes contained in cardboard boxes and for the first time we 'draw and fit' a parachute we will jump with. With everyone helping his nearest mate to get 'rigged up' each main and reserve parachute has a number stencilled onto it which is logged with the name and service number of the man using it. It's extremely time consuming.

Below each of the balloons is tethered to an oblong shaped steel box known as the cage, which is roughly the size of the back of an open Land Rover. Each balloon is attached via a steel cable to a winch lorry, when the winch is released the balloon and cage ascends to eight hundred feet carrying four trainees and their instructor. One at a time the men jump leading to a drop of two hundred feet before the parachute canopy becomes fully deployed.

With the paperwork complete you sit in rows four deep and using fitted parachutes as back rests watch as the first cage rises into the heavens. It takes ages for the first man to jump and when he does, a split second later the shouted order to GO reaches us. Initially just a dot falling like a stone, the parachute lazily blossoms open and an instructor on the ground begins giving flight and landing instructions via a loud hailer. When numbers two and three jump time drags on until the winch begins hauling the balloon down, someone murmurs.

"Number four has refused.

He's right, the instant the balloon lands a blue Land Rover appears and speeds to meet it. The man who's refused has his main and reserve parachutes removed and he's promptly driven away never to be seen again. For everyone it's very distressing to witness.

By now the second balloon is operational and things speed up considerably. Suddenly your instructor walks toward you rubbing his hands together as he gleefully shouts.

"Come'on my lot!" Your butterflies, crouching pensively in your stomach, instantly rear up as four of you stand up and follow your instructor to the waiting cage. Entering it, he takes each man's static line, an immensely strong length of tan coloured webbing which pulls the parachute open and attaches it to a strong point just above the open gap or doorway of the cage. Being number three you go to the far-left hand corner. Giving each static line a hard tug on the strong point the instructor shouts. "One OK - two OK-?" etc...

When all four mumble "Yes!" he shouts to the winch crew.

"Up eight hundred - four men jumping!"

Placing a steel safety bar across the open gap, which is the exit door, the instructor folds his arms and casually leans against it. When the winch begins droning allowing the monstrous balloon to lift off, it doesn't stay parallel with the ground as you expect, instead it tilts forward at a sickening angle compelling everyone to lean back and hold on very tightly as you gaze down enviously at your mates walking off the drop zone carrying rolled up parachute canopies in their arms. As you ascend higher they gradually become smaller and smaller. When the cage finally levels off it begins swaying slightly. Your instructor breaks the deathly silence when he comments. "Come on lads, cheer up, if this thing was in a fairground, you'd have to pay for a go on it!" You all force a smile, but nobody speaks.

Suddenly the distant drone of the winch grinds to a halt and an ominous silence confirming the cage has arrived at eight hundred feet. Perhaps you look down at a distant motorway, a mere pencil line winding across the brown and green terrain showing tiny moving dots where normal people do normal things. You may catch a glimpse of your hand gripping the side of the cage, your knuckles brilliant white. Peering down with all the calm of one who might be casually examining his shoes, your instructor, with an inevitable grin declares.

JOURNEY TO PRAGUE AND OTHER MILEAGE   11

"We're on lads! We've got the green flag!" He removes the safety bar, which is connected to a short chain, drops it into the corner behind him and with devastating politeness comments.

"Number one, into the door please!" Number one steps into the open gap and grasping steel uprights either side of it waits for the command. "Prepare for action!" Instantly he brings one arm down to rest on the top of his reserve parachute. Locked in a world of his own, he stares straight ahead when the instructor shouts. "Action stations!" When Number one drops his other arm down the instructor shouts "Gooowww!" and with no hesitation whatsoever he steps into the waiting void. Watching him descend, the instructor murmurs "Very nicely done indeed!"

Hoisting Number one's static line and the outer bag of his parachute into the cage, he drops it into the corner behind him and grinning at an ashen faced Number two invites him to step into the open gap. When he jumps the instructor looks at you and nods saying quietly.

"Into the door Number three!"

Walking toward that wide open gap from the back of the cage it seems the longest few steps in the world, but at no time do you hesitate, by now you have a mindset where you will either walk off that DZ but never leave it in a blue Land Rover. Standing in the doorway you fleetingly glance down at the dinky sized winch lorry, your stomach churns like never before.

"Prepare for action!" Commands a voice beside you. When you instantly obey you hear.

"Action stations, followed immediately by "Gooowww!" Stepping briskly into thin air your knees and feet automatically join together and as your butterflies stampede from your stomach to your throat you look up to see rigging lines growing out of your shoulder noisily tearing themselves free to become an enormous white, thirty-two feet diameter lifesaving dome which billows out and begins to breathe, opening and closing slightly as it fills with air. Then, you're gently floating down amid an explosion of sudden elation which expunges all else, most of all the instructor with the megaphone. As the ground comes rushing up you touch down and immediately roll. The ground instructor comes striding toward you saying advisedly. "I know how you feel son, we all do on the first descent, but do try to listen to my instructions, parachuting is a very serious business!"

Nodding vigorously you exclaim. "Yes Flight!" He then adds.

"Get yourself a cup of tea, you'll be back up there before you know it!"

Turning and banging the circular release box at your midriff to unlock the parachute couplings, you see Number four approaching who's ex 3 para now in the reserves. When he asks what you think about your first parachute descent your answer is immediate and totally honest when you answer. "Now I know why selection was such a pure bastard! You've got to want to do it!" He grins and nods. On your second descent you jump with much more confidence and the return journey back to the camp is in stark contrast to the one coming out.

Wolfing down your evening meal and singing our heads off in the showers, you change into jeans and tee shirts and head for the camp club where the juke box belts out the hit song of the day, 'Puppy Love' by Donny Osmond. Nobody mentions the rolled-up mattress and the empty locker of the man who refused to jump, he's long since left the base. You raise your glass to him and quietly wish him the best of luck. In the forthcoming days you learn to exit amid the roaring noise of the mighty C130 in what your instructors call fun jumps, meaning you don't jump with heavy equipment containers. In what they casually term 'Slightly more demanding' your determination is stretched even further when you do so. The final reward comes with a parade where the base commander hands you parachute wings and shakes your hand. You can't wait to sew them on upper right shoulder of your smock.

You're now an airborne soldier...

CHAPTER THREE

LAWNMOWER MEN

Autumn – 1970

Following four weeks' absence due to severe bronchial illness I was looking forward to getting back to the factory where I work only to be told I will doing light duties for a few weeks. The factory is renowned for its generosity and consideration to employees, at Christmas the children of workers attend a party in the factory canteen where each one receives a quality present. One year, due to excess profits, every employee was paid one hundred pounds as a gift from management. It is an amazing place to work and typically light duties on something called 'The Presentation Squad' is meant to ease men back into work after long absences.

It sounded good until I discover light duties means cleaning toilets, so there I am walking around the factory carrying a bucket filled with bottles of bleach and disinfectants plus a mop with a handle ideal for carrying spare rolls of toilet paper. It takes roughly ten minutes each to clean the four toilets allotted to me three time a day, otherwise the work is immensely boring. The boss of the squad is Mr. Briggs, an overweight, bald-headed man who's basically an office worker who's instructed to keep an eye on the squad. Bereft of anything resembling a sense of humour he thrives on his newfound authority. The factory owns a nearby sports field which includes a bowling green and a small pavilion that's occasionally hired out to factory personnel for wedding receptions and birthday parties etc. When Mr. Briggs orders me and another cleaner named John to go to the pavilion and clean it following a wedding party, he adds we can also sweep up the autumn leaves layering the bowling green and put them into bin liners. John is roughly my age, slightly bigger than me and very easy going. Feeling blessed to get away from the noisy pulsations of the factory we set off for the twenty-minute walk to the sports field and unlocking the pavilion door see on the small internal bar half full bottles of spirits, wine, and several six packs of beer. Nestling beside them are several cardboard plates with cling film covering sandwiches and rolls overflowing with cooked meat. John grins, murmuring. "Fancy a drink and a bite to eat Bar?"

"Why not?" I reply, unable to recall the last time I had a drink of any kind. Helping ourselves to a few sandwiches and washing them down with generous snorts from the bottles of spirits half an hour later the middle-aged woman who enters the pavilion can't fail to see two empty cardboard plates and two slightly pixilated men. Curtly refusing our assistance to help her she walks back and forth from the pavilion to her car collecting all the food and fluid remnants of the wedding then, giving us a stern glare that would melt snow she gets into the car, slams the door, and drives off. John, somewhat panicked, begins to relax when I assure him all we can do is finish cleaning the pavilion and the bowling green and hope she turns a blind eye. Pausing only to relieve straining bladders we feverishly clean the pavilion and carrying bin liners plus the only available sweeping brush begin gathering up millions of leaves layering the immense bowling green which is as time consuming as emptying a swimming pool with a bucket. With time running out when we should be on our way back to the factory to clock out, and aware we have the keys to the nearby groundman's shed, when I suggest using a lawnmower to effectively hoover up the leaves John immediately agrees. Unlocking the shed we see several large lawn mowers and picking the biggest one push it over to the bowling green which is recessed inside a foot high surrounding grass embankment. Roughly handling the mower onto the bowling green John pulls a cord tied around a wooden handle to start the engine which fires up but refuses to keep going. When I see a curved lever on the handlebars with the word 'choke' on it I push it wide open and when John tries again there comes a sudden explosion of black smoke and before we can stop it the lawnmower goes careering across the bowling throwing lumps of grass out from both sides and collides with the distant embankment where it coughs and splutters a few times before fading to deathly silence. Staring in muted disbelief at the livid brown scar across what moments earlier was a meticulously perfect bowling green I murmur incredulously.

"Bloody hell?" With my comment jerking us out of our statue like disbelief we run over to the lawnmower and promptly lift it out of the bowling green then, with both our expressions frozen masks of increasing panic we begin making frantic repairs by scooping up pieces of mangled lawn we place over the scar and compress into place with our boots. The result is like trying to conceal an elephant under a tablecloth. When it occurs to me we must surely look like something straight out of a Laurel and Hardy Movie I pick up a piece of turf and gently pressing it into place with my boot say to John whose kneeling beside me.

"I think this bit fits here, what do you think?" Nodding, but not saying a word, when he places a saucer sized piece of turf beside mine and looks at me as though seeking my approval, I snatch it up and move it a few inches saying.

"John, are you blind? ARE YOU BLIND? Anyone can see...?" Suddenly overwhelmed with such uncontrollable laughter I simply can't speak, after several attempts I finally manage to say. "Anyone can see it the bloody thing fit's better where I put it!" As the sheer absurdity of what we're trying to do erupts into contagious mutual laughter all it takes to explode over and over is eye contact and more ham-fisted but hilarious debate about what piece fits where. By now virtually helpless with mirth, with simmering belligerence a nearby voice suddenly bellows. "What-the-bleeding-hell-is-going-on-here?" In sudden silence you could cut with a scalpel we see Mr. Briggs standing near the pavilion with his legs apart and both hands resting on his hips closely resembling Captain Bligh on the quarter deck of the Bounty about to have us both flogged. When I glance at John, who's wide open mouth looks as if he's trying to swallow an invisible orange, I burst into laughter enraging Captain Bligh as he vengefully rants.

"This is willful damage to company property, AND I've received a complaint you've both been drinking! Get that machine back into the shed and lock everything up, you're both in serious trouble, be in my office nine am in the morning!" Inflicting a parting hateful glower at us he turns and walks away. Suddenly it's not funny anymore. Walking back to the factory and clocking out we agree we are almost certainly going to be sacked. The next morning Mr. Briggs curtly informs us he is suspending us for two weeks while he considers what to do with us, rumour has it he's influenced by the grounds man who would love to see us hung, drawn and quartered. When the two-week suspension ends, not unexpectedly we receive a letter signed by Mr. Briggs stating our employment at the factory is now terminated. Then, when all seems hopeless, to our rescue comes Jim Watson, a shop steward, a solid, old fashioned union man who feels we have been punished with two weeks suspension and to also sack us is surely to punish us twice. When he launches an appeal to higher management another letter arrives stating we are to see the manager of the factory at ten am the next morning, his name is Mr. Hill, word has it he's a former Parachute Regiment Officer, he will make the final decision. When John and I, wearing our best suits and both highly pensive as we stand outside Mr. Hill's office things begin to happen when Mr. Briggs strides pompously toward us and ignores us when he speaks to Miss Johnson, an attractive secretary who smiles, speaks into her intercom then tells him to enter the office. Emerging moments later he gruffly orders us to enter. As apprehensive as I feel, poor John looks like he's halfway up the steps to a guillotine. The office is palatial. Wearing a pin striped suit Mr. Hill sits behind a huge desk and without saying a word imparts an aura of immense authority. To look at he is not unlike the actor George Sanders and proves to have the same velvet, highly articulate voice. Standing and glancing at each of us he comes to the front of his desk and folding his arms leans against it murmuring.

"Thank you, Mr. Briggs, that will be all!"

As John and I glance at Mr. Briggs radiating an air of ravenous expectancy, obviously amazed he is being dismissed he makes no move to leave and when he begins to say something Mr. Hill looks directly at him and with slow very curt emphasis commands.

"That will be all Briggs!" With his demeanor changing from Captain Bligh to Uriah Heep, I wonder if he's going to bow when he pulls the door open. The instant it closes Mr. Hill comments. "Now then gentleman, you're accused of drinking on duty and causing willful damage to company property, before I decide what to do with you, I'd like to hear your account of exactly what happened?"

John and I glance knowingly at each other, we have agreed I will do the talking. When Mr. Hill returns behind his desk and sits down. Well aware this man only has to blink and we're both headed for the dole queue I begin by politely explaining how we were sent to clean up the pavilion and the bowling green and how we saw the food and drinks and assumed nobody would mind if we had a bite to eat and a quick drink, 'to toast the bride'. Mr. Hill nods and blessedly does not ask me to elaborate. Explaining how we cleaned the pavilion then decided the most efficient way to clean the leaves on the bowling green was to use a lawn mower as a hoover he listens and occasionally nods but when I begin to describe how the lawnmower fired up and escaped across the bowling green I'm powerless to stop graphic pictures appearing on the screen of my mind's eye and when I briefly glance at John, staring down at his feet to conceal he's in a worse state of impending laughter than I am, his beseeching grimace when we make fleeting eye contact silently pleads.

"NOT NOW BARRIE, for God's sake NOT NOW!" Only with a herculean effort do I continue. "I don't wish to make light of the damage we did sir, but it was an accident, we did our best to repair to the bowling green!" That's it, dole queue or not I can't keep a straight face or contain laughter for another second, neither can John who visibly shudders. Mr. Hill, seemingly engrossed in the story, enquires.

"What do you mean, repair the bowling green?" It is all I can do to mumble.

"We were in such panic when we saw the brown scar left by the lawnmower, we began putting bits of turf over it to repair it, but when we began arguing what piece fitted where it just became so hilariously funny, we simply couldn't stop laughing, that's when Mr. Briggs arrived!" Mr. Hill gives a slight cough and ominously enquires.

"I see, and have you both lost two weeks' pay?"

"Yes sir!" We reply in tandem.

"A pretty expensive drink, wouldn't you say!"

"Yes sir!" We repeat.

Taking a few moments where he's obviously trying not to smile, he states.

"Well, I see no malicious intent here, the fact is you got carried away and got caught, the thing I find most in your favour, not to mention amusing, is your attempt to repair the damage you did!" With no sign of his previous humour his eyes slowly narrow, his voice very brusque when he adds.

"OK. I will not take this any further, you can return to your jobs but get into trouble again and you are out, understood!"

"Yes sir!" We exclaim.

Even more emphatically he adds.

"One more thing, the matter ends here, if anybody, whatever their position, makes any trouble whatsoever, you come directly to me and I will personally sort them out, is that clearly understood?" Knowing he's referring to an office worker who believes he can sack people, in another spontaneous echo we exclaim. "Yes sir!"

"Right, off you go, and gentlemen...?" Pausing and gazing down at something on his desk he murmurs. "Stay away from lawn mowers!" Mumbling our thanks, we leave his office where we receive a broad smile from Miss Johnson and a glowering gaze from Bligh before the intercom buzzes and he's summoned into the office. Back to cleaning toilets before taking up our regular factory jobs, with events now common knowledge to some workmates, those who think inside a thimble, we are infamous vandals to be shunned on sight, however the vast majority greet us by inquiring if we could possibly, 'Mow their lawns next Saturday!'

CHAPTER FOUR

THE AMERICAN WAY...

March 1973

The only time I ever experienced an aborted parachute descent came when I was on attachment as medic to 10 Para, a reservist airborne unit. As part of a huge weekend exercise it was a night jump where three times they got us into the door psyched up ready to go and three times the red light stayed until a throat-cutting gesture from the senior Flight Sergeant confirmed the jump was scrubbed. We never found out what the problem was but being diverted to RAF Mildenhall we're ordered to wait for transport to catch up with the rest of the exercise. So began a night to remember...

Disembarking the Hercules laden with kit and faces full of Cammy cream, an officer with a broad American accent pulls up in a jeep and suggests we make our way to the camp club for a beer. It's a Friday evening and hearing pulsating Disco music in the distance we head toward it. Detailing two guys to guard a small mountain of the jump containers gear we enter the camp club and removing our berets walk up to the bar where, exactly like one of those westerns where the bad guy walks into the saloon the music begins to dwindle and the large American contingent in the camp stare at us as if we're from another planet. When a guy asks one of our sergeants who we are, and he states we're British paratroopers waiting for transport after an aborted night drop, our cousins from over the pond change from curiosity to unbridled hospitality as they crowd around us wanting to know our names amid offers to buy our berets, the bar is thrown open and when someone inquires if we're hungry a group of us are invited to a canteen where we tuck into fries and huge steaks layered with onions we saturate with Worcester Sauce. From waiting to exit on a night jump to this unexpected immensely enjoyable few hours care of Americans there came a humorous ending when trucks arrived at the front gate and a young officer tried to explain to a black female Sergeant who he was and what he was doing there. Apparently she promptly shoved a 9ml Browning into his face and cocked it gruffly stating.

"Buster - you ain't going nowhere until I find out who you are, now get your arse outta this truck and follow me!" Taking him to the guardhouse clearance to enter was eventually given.

The next day, rejoining the exercise, I'm lying under a bush between two machine gunners freezing cold and so tired every time I blink my eyes slam shut. Thinking about those fries and those enormous steaks I turn the key on that much sought after delicacy in the British Army, a tin of corned beef. RAF Mildenhall. A glimpse into the American way that would never have happened if that night jump hadn't been aborted...

CHAPTER FIVE

AIRBORNE MOVIE EXTRA'S

Kyrenia Castle – Northern Cyprus

Cyprus 1973

When our C/O announces three weeks in Cyprus are up for grabs for what will be continuous day and night parachuting there is no shortage of applicants for those who can get the time off work. First to apply are my two best mates Brian and Mac and before we know it we're on our way to the jewel of the Med billeted in Alexandra Barracks in Dhekelia which has cream coloured buildings and red tiled roofs meant to resemble the closed shields of a Roman Legion. Immediately outside the camp gate is a mobile food van run by an amiable Greek who cooks the most incredible fried egg rolls, when he's not playing 'Zorba the Greek' on his cassette recorder he's playing top of the chart hits such as, 'Dueling Banjos' from the Movie 'Deliverance' and 'Killing me Softly' by Roberta Flack.

Now on attachment to 2 Para, an RAF liaison officer tells us we will be parachuting clean fatigue (no equipment containers) for new Hercules pilots to experience dropping airborne troops. Incredibly, the middle week will be time off to do anything we choose. The pilots very generously send over several crates of beer. The following day we drive in convoy to a huge hanger in Nicosia Airport where we meet a dozen or so parachute packers from RAF Hullavinton whose job is to collect and repack the parachutes after each drop. When parachuting begins we're up and down like yo-yo's. As soon as we land trucks immediately take us back to 'Nickers' where we draw and fit and take off again. The weather is faultless, the whole deal is a repetitive, though demanding breeze.

The first week passes with plenty of jumps logged and no incidents. When the week off arrives, Brian, Mac, me and a regular named Mark hire a car to tour the island, a Ford Anglia costing a phenomenal twelve pounds for five days. Taking sleeping bags, towels, bathers and shaving gear etc we set out to visit the Troodos Mountains and stop anywhere that appears even remotely interesting, one being a roadside restaurant where one of the dining tables is perched in a tree. The food is delicious and unbelievably cheap; our favourite being Calamari (Squid) and chips. Accommodation is never a problem, in what we call 'Staying at the Sandy Beach Hotel' we simply find the nearest secluded beach, roll out our sleeping bags and crash out. Away from the gruelling day and night descents our priority, to relax and unwind is never without humour. Toward the end of the week we arrive at a small coastal town called Kyrenia which has a huge castle perched beside a picturesque harbour surrounded by pulsating Bars and Café's. We soon learn an Arab Dhow moored in the harbour is being used to make a Movie called 'Ghost in the Noonday Sun' starring Peter Sellers, Spike Milligan and Tony Franciosa.. Sitting around a table in a quayside Taverna watching the world go by a guy carrying a clip board approaches us and inquires if we're soldiers. "We're Airborne!" Replies Mark indignantly.

"Paratroopers, that's excellent!" The man exclaims, quickly adding. "How would you like to be in this Movie?" More than a little agog we glance at each other.

"What would we have to do?" Asks Brian, who has a unique personality where nothing ruffles his easy-going demeanour and permanently wide grin. If something does it's best to get well clear of him. The Movie guy pulls up a seat and continues.

"We're doing a scene when its dark, a few people, stunt men portraying the actors, will escape from the castle by climbing down the castle wall on ropes, what I need are four men to stand on guard while the escape takes place, you will all given Arab costumes, I'll pay you five pounds each for little more than half an hour's work, interested?" While three of us conceal our growing enthusiasm that twenty quid will help pay for the car not to mention several slap-up meals, young Mac, who's very good looking, generous to a fault and from my experience of night ballooning with him, utterly fearless, gazes at each of us stating with his usual inherent honesty.

"Hang on guys, are we sure we can do this when we're in the British Army?"

As three pairs of eyes scowl fleeting daggers at Mac silently beseeching him to shut the f... to say nothing more, he lapses into silence.

"OK!" Says Brian. "You've got four guards, what do we do now?"

The guy takes out his wallet, removes a small card and writes on the back of it.

'Four Arabs with rifles' Handing it to Brian he points and saying.

"Follow that road over there, you will come to a large white hotel, you can't miss it, go inside, go down to the basement to our wardrobe department, give this card to the man you see there, he'll do the rest, meet me you back here when its dark and I'll tell you what to do, any questions?"

"Yeah, when do we get paid?" I murmur curiously. He smiles and answers.

"Immediately the shot is finished, you hand in your costumes at the Hotel and get your money, is it a deal?"

"It's a deal!" We reply. Amid this unexpected wealth coming our way we have a few more beers before casually walking to the hotel. In the basement, where hundreds of differing costumes hang from endless rows of mobile rails the man we meet makes no effort to hide he has big eyes for young Mac. "Hmm..." He murmurs, devouring Mac with ravenous, undisguised lust. "WHAT... have we got here?" When Brian passes over the card he places one hand on his hip, the other to his mouth gazing around saying.

"What have I got to turn such lovely boys like yourselves into four Arabs?" Then, positively drooling at Mac he adds, "I've got just the thing, especially for you my darling!" Mac, crimson and cringing, doesn't know where to look. Half an hour later we emerge from the hotel carrying horrendously long wooden rifles looking like four horrible versions of Laurence of Arabia.. Over our shorts and tee shirts we're draped from head to toe in black robes with enormous hoods, most hilarious of all are long black beards held in place by lengths of elastic stretching over our heads and concealed under the hoods. Beginning to get dark as we walk back to the harbour, Brian, who has the devil in him, approaches a middle-aged couple festooned with cameras and standing in front of them furtively gazes in all directions before saying. "Do you VANT to buy some dirty photographs?" Watching and creaking with laughter, everything goes wrong when the man, indignant he's being accosted, or possibly mugged becomes very hostile compelling Brian to diffuse him by removing his hood and beard then reassuring him we're not muggers we're paras dressed as film extras. As quick as the man winds up, he winds down, grins, and even takes our picture. (What I wouldn't give for a copy!). Resuming our walk to the harbour, Brian doesn't try selling anymore 'dirty photographs'.

Arriving at the quayside Taverna, our 'employer' is anxiously waiting for us and leads us to the far side of the harbour to a long jetty directly opposite the castle where several glowing steel braziers are roughly six feet apart. Placing each of us beside a brazier he informs us we're to stand with our rifles leaning slightly forward and with huge emphasis adds we're to do nothing, say nothing and stand absolutely still while the scene is being shot.

"No sweat!" We all echo. By now it's completely dark and minutes later a voice behind a loudhailer suddenly commands something to the effect. "OK! Quiet on the set! Escape Scene, roll-em!"

Facing the castle like four rigid statues and not failing to miss figures climbing down the walls I hear Mark murmur with irrefutable logic. "Any boy scout with a catapult could take these dickheads out!" Stifling a chuckle I glance at Mac who's no doubt speculating what will happen if we're caught 'moonlighting' from the British Army. That leaves Brian. Turning my head a fraction I can't believe what I'm seeing when he pulls his beard down and mumbles. "Hiya Mam!" It's so hilarious and so typical of him my robes and the five feet long rifle begin to tremble. Luckily the camera is now concentrating on the stuntmen who get safely to the ground and run off. Then, blessedly, the booming voice behind the loudhailer shouts. "Cut - OK - That's it for now folks - there's a food wagon arriving shortly - Everyone help yourself!" As the harbour gradually comes back to life I walk over to Brian stating with mammoth affection. "That was outrageous!"

"True!" He responds with an inevitable broad grin. By the time we get back to the landside of the harbour a huge chuck wagon has arrived and along with the crew we help ourselves to a seemingly endless supply of hot dogs and hamburgers. Returning the costumes and receiving a crisp five-pound note each we tour the bars of Kyrenia where many show signed photographs of famous actors, one bar displays military cap badges from virtually every army in the world, including Russia. We have a fabulous evening talking to members of the set, but don't meet any of the stars. Collecting our sleeping bags from the car we wander over to a gate of the castle near to where the Dhow, now departed, was berthed. The guy who hired us told us we could crash out there, but we're awakened in the small hours by a torch shining into our faces. Half asleep and sitting up in our sleeping bags we stare at a Greek policeman wearing a peaked cap who begins ranting in broken English we must move on, explaining we're film extras with permission to bunk down on the set he's not remotely interested. When he swings forward a Sterling SMG, concealed behind his back on a shoulder sling, he cocks it, leans very businesslike into it and gruffly orders us to move, or he'll fire. Brian, not missing glaring impending defiance from Mac, myself and Mark, instantly takes charge when he suddenly bellows. "That's it, we're moving, get your gear! NAW!" When he puts that bite into his voice a statue would obey. Cursing and shivering we roll up our sleeping bags, pull on our trainers and leave our snug little recess. We've done nothing wrong, but discretion must be the better part of valour. Following a short distance behind us pointing the SMG at us, young Mac, fearless Mac turns and wagging a finger at the policeman states with classic piss taking humour.

"We'll see what Peter Sellers has got to say about this!" We're all suddenly grinning as we gather Mac to us and drive to the nearest Sandy

Beach Hotel. It's a pointedly bad ending to an otherwise excellent day. The next morning we clean the car before returning it. A day later we're back parachuting and there follows a week of very hairy descents where two men finish up in the BMH - British Military Hospital. On a final night descent our parachute packers come up with us to watch the exits. I jump number two, close enough to the door to see a tiny circle of lights far below marking the drop zone. Number one is a Sergeant. When we land, the illuminated circle is huge yet little more than tins with flickering flames inside them. The Sergeant and I are so close to them when we touch down we must rapidly pull our canopies clear of the markers because they're in danger of touching the flames. In a parachute drop of absolute pinpoint accuracy we walk side by side off the DZ. The pilots can remove their L plates. Suddenly it's time for an end of course party before returning home to the normality of work and everyday life. In the drill hall the following Wednesday I read the standing orders notice board and learn to my delight I've been promoted to Lance Corporal.

Tragically, later in the year an item on 'News at Ten' shows Turkish Paras dropping onto Cyprus where that fabulous Island paradise descends into all-out war ending in a demarcation zone separating North from South. It remains so to this day...

CHAPTER SIX

MILITARY HUMOUR...

Soldiers, whoever they - wherever they are - whatever their unit, thrive on unrelenting black humour...
It comes with the job.

A General walks into a field hospital filled with wounded soldiers. He stops at the bed of the first soldier and asks what happened. The soldier replies...

"Sir - I wus in my trench when we wus attacked! A grenade landed by my feet - when I picked it up to throw it back it exploded and blew off my hand - but I can't wait to get my false hand and get back up the line with all my mates sir!"

The General smiles saying... "Good man - jolly good show - jolly jolly good show!"

He moves on and asks the next wounded soldier what happened.

The soldier replies... "Sir - I wus on patrol and we wus mortared - blew one of my legs off, but I can't wait to get my tin leg and get back up the line with all my mates sir!"

The General smiles saying. "Good man - jolly good show - jolly jolly good show!"

Moving on the General comes to a bed with curtains around it. He steps inside them and is amazed to see that on the pillow is a head - nothing else - just a head.

The General can't believe what he's seeing - says curiously,

"My goodness - what on earth happened to you?"

The head opens its eyes, looks up and promptly says "Piss off!"

The General replies... "Look here old chap - you really can't speak to me like that I'm a General!"

"I don't give a monkey's who you are!" Says the head angrily. "Piss off!"

The General quickly leaves and spots a medical orderly - saying "The morale of these wounded men is really outstanding - but that chappie at the top of the ward - the one behind the curtains - he was very rude to me – very rude indeed - he told me to go away and use the toilet - I'm thinking of putting him on a charge?"

"That's Private Bloggs sir!" Says the orderly. "He's not having a very good day - in fact sir - he's just had some very bad news - very bad news indeed!"

"Really - in what way?" Asks the General.

"Well sir - this morning we put him on a wheelchair and took him to see the Optician - it looks like he will have to wear glasses!"

"That's terrible!" says the General. The orderly adds. "It's worse than that sir - on the way back from the Opticians we took him in to see the Ear Specialist - it looks like he's going to need a hearing aids!"

"Oh that poor chap - what terribly bad luck - I can see why he's not very happy!" exclaims the General. The orderly shakes his head and then adds...

"That's not all sir - before we came back here we popped him in to see the Dentist, he's got to have all his teeth out!"

CHAPTER SEVEN

SCORPIONS – SHARKS – AND SNAKES

Pre-jump Manifest UAE 1973

United Arab Emirates
1973

Children are children wherever they are...

As a unit of airborne reservists on a six-week exercise in the UAE we drive in convoy through isolated villages where kids stand beside the road waving excitedly as we throw them sweets from our 24-hour ration packs. In stark contrast their mothers never fail to cover their faces and turn away. In one village where we stop to stretch our legs an eight feet long shark is stretched out on a wooden table for villagers to watch it being carved up and shared out. As sleek and shiny as they appear, touching the skin of a shark is like touching very coarse sandpaper. Declining the offer of buying bits of the shark we thank the villagers and move out.

Rotating between three locations, Wadi Shawkah, Ras Diba and Manama, the best thing about our new location is how close it is to the sea. The camps itself consists of a line of well weathered brown tents known as bivy's housing four men and a few airborne shelters which are extremely well-constructed from canvas and aluminium framework. In the distance are latrine tents and a large communal tent with benches where we swap yans and enjoy the two cans of beer were allowed each day. An Arab trader who occasionally visits, sells bits and pieces such as nail cutters with a small knife blade built into the handle. Everyone buys one.

Our task is to patrol the area and get to know both the locals and the terrain. The sun is shining, we can swim when time allows and the camp appears to be a good place to spend a few days, but beneath the surface lurks the totally unexpected. Soon after we settle in I spot a loose tent peg at the side of my bivvy, nearby are some round heavy rocks, picking one up to bang in the tent peg I experience a sudden surge of fear and revulsion arrives when I see a scorpion crawl from beneath the rock and pause between my hands and at the same time I feel my hair tingle I tip-up the scorpion onto the ground to give it a terminal headache with the same rock. Because several men see what happened word soon gets around about 'Taffy's Scorpion'.

Matters are not helped when later that day one of our guys pulls his sleeping bag from the top of his tent where it's been placed to air and a small snake falls to the ground. To any soldier the only good snake is a dead one and it's mercilessly bumped off. Following these events everything that moves, slithers, crawls, grunts, groans or farts is suspected of being sinister y setting the stage for a quite unbelievable sequence of events.

Two thousand years earlier our Sergeant Major would undoubtedly have been a Centurion in the Roman Army knocking the lights out of any soldier who didn't instantly obey him. About five feet ten inches tall he wears SAS para wings and is the kind of man other men measure themselves by. With a permanently grizzled expression and deeply etched skin not unlike a worn-out leather handbag, it's a face that has banqueted on life itself.

Taking a shine to me possibly because, as an attachment medic I'm the only Welshman in what is predominantly a Scottish section of the unit he refers to me as Taff. Shortly after the scorpion episode he approaches my bivy as I'm preparing breakfast on my Hexi stove and asks if I can swim.

"Like a fish Boss!" I reply, handing him my mug of freshly made tea.

"Ever done any scuba diving?" He asks. When I shake my head, he comments.

"Fancy learning?"

When I rapidly exclaim. "Boss - does a goose crap?" He points, saying.

"That airborne shelter's full of divers from 9 Squadron RE, attach yourself to them for the rest of the day, tell them I sent you. and Taff, stay switched on, they don't take prisoners!"

Handing back my mug he walks away. Half an hour later, wearing bathers, shorts, flip flops, and my SMG draped over my shoulder I walk over to the airborne shelter to see the roof covered with sleeping bags and the surrounding area festooned with diving equipment. Dressed exactly like me and lounging around outside are half a dozen men who are deeply suntanned with not an ounce of fat between them. Introducing myself, saying who sent me and why, they amenably invite me to 'Grab a pew' beside a guy who's leafing through a large book showing coloured pictures of horrendous shark attacks on both fish and humans. Following much easy-going banter, we load copious amounts of diving gear into a trailer and hitching it behind a Land Rover drive about half a mile to the coast.

At the water's edge one of the men passes me the top half of a wet suit and explains the basic rules of scuba diving, the first one being I will have two professional divers beside me and under no circumstances am I to panic while submerged. By now another guy placing an air tank to my back hands me a pair of fins curtly telling me 'Never call them flippers'. I'm taught and made to repeat several hand signals and finally an extremely heavy belt made from squares of solid lead is secured around my waist in place held there by a quick release pin. With an instructor either side of me we enter the sea walking backward into it and when the water reaches my waist copying my instructors, I dip my face mask in the water and rub spittle on the inside of the glass, only then do I see a guy perched high in some nearby rocks with a rifle across his knees intently scanning the sea through a pair of binoculars. When I casually inquire what he is doing, one of the instructor's glances at him and replies. "He's the Shark watcher, it's not a sweat, the chances of seeing one are extremely remote!"

Reluctant to mention I saw an eight feet long shark on a table in a coastal village, when we all plunge underwater I immediately discover breathing via an air tank is initially cumbersome but quickly becomes second nature. Swimming out to sea we enter a world of indescribable colour where shoals of colourful fish, thousands in number, hover in the gentle current, when bolder one's swim close to the glass of my face mask they retreat with lightning speed when I instinctively reach out to touch them. Every few minutes one of my instructors nudges me and holds up his thumb, meaning. 'Are you OK?' I respond with a raised thumb. 'Yes!' Languishing on the ocean bed are such items as a long-abandoned anchor and the barnacle encrusted hull of a boat that has seen better days. Utterly transfixed by this totally new experience I lose all track of time until I'm nudged by an instructor making frantic upward pointing movements meaning. 'Get to the surface immediately'. Behind his face mask his eyes bulge with obvious alarm. Seconds later all three of us are treading water on the surface where he pushes his mask onto his forehead and exclaims with considerable urgency. "There's a shark in the area!" His partner, gazing furtively in all directions, suddenly points to a spot a few hundred yards away and shouts guardedly. "There he is, he's just gone under!" Feeling acutely vulnerable when he pulls the pin on my weights belt, which instantly falls away, he begins releasing my air tank from my shoulders, stating in a controlled emphatic voice.

"LISTEN IN MATE, swim back to the shore, DON'T RUSH, nothing will attract a shark faster than a panicked swimmer. Take your time, is that clear?"

"Yes!" I splutter. "What about you two?" He shouts back.

"If he comes this way we'll be watching your back, start heading back in!"

In the time it takes to look at the shore, not an inch less than a quarter of a mile away, I turn back to see that both men have swum a short distance from me where they urgently scan the open sea. When one of them glances at my hesitancy he brusquely shouts.

"For Christ's sake man, get back to shore!"

Being neither the time nor the place to argue, with long over arm strokes hauling me forward in perfect unison with the steady rhythmic peddling of my fins I begin the most terrifying swim of my entire life with my thoughts a sizzling cauldron of keeping a tight lid on my fear until I recall the Sergeant Major's comment. 'Stay switched on, they don't take prisoners!" Taking precious seconds to pause and look back but seeing nothing except harmless empty sea with no sign of my instructors or a shark I begin to relax when I figure this has got to be a set up, but when I see distant figures on the shore shouting and frantically waving followed by an unmistakable puff of smoke from the rifle of the Shark watcher I resume swimming fit to earn a gold medal until I finally scramble onto land and sagging breathlessly down into hot sand tear off my face mask to see the men either bent double, stretched flat out or sat with their heads between their knees prior to a collective eruption of laughter. A short distance out in the surf one of my instructors is holding my air tank, the other my weights belt. Hoisting their masks above their foreheads both are broadly grinning as I look the shark-watcher mumbling incredulously. "But…you shot at something behind me?" It takes a few moments for his mirth to subside before he states with huge amusement. "Blanks!" All I can do is grin when I'm informed I've now completed a standard initiation for a new diver.

I'm soon back underwater again with one eye open for a 'Shark'.

When we finish for the day and load up the trailer, for no other reason than to reflect on my 'standard initiation for a new diver' when I tell my mates I'd like to walk back to the camp, one of them hands me my SMG and still grinning they drive off. It's a fabulously tranquil evening and rather than using the dirt track back to the camp I begin walking up the coastline enjoying the warm surf that washes over my flip-flops. On a far horizon the sun is gently sinking behind a distant mountain range while swathing the land with a tranquil orange glow as if turning down the dimmer switch on another day. It's a perfectly idyllic moment on a day I will never forget, but as I'm about to turn inland toward the camp a vague movement further up the beach catches my eye. Curious enough to walk briskly towards it I'm astounded to see thousands of land crabs with spectacular colours on their shells crawling up the beach making a slight drone as their pincers scrape against each other. When hundreds stop in self-surviving silence as they sense my footsteps, such is the appeal of those shells, I decide to get some. Nearby I spot an ideal container, a washed ashore bin liner.

It's dark when I finally walk into the camp, wrapped tightly inside the bin liner are roughly a dozen crabs. Placing it in my tent under my sleeping bag I get a brew and my evening scoff up and running. Carrying my SMG and joining the men in the beer tent I take in my stride the inevitable ragging I receive for being 'the para who tried to outswim a shark'. Swapping yarns and making our ration of beer last as long as possible we wander back to our bivy's, strip down to our shorts and clamber into sleeping bags. All four of us settle down to sleep but the absolute silence is broken in the wee small hours when one of my Scottish mates awakens to the distinct sound of 'things' crawling around the floor. Roughly shaking me awake he shouts. "Wake up Taff - WAKE UP - Get out of here, the tent is crawling with scorpions!" Scrambling to our feet we all charge through the tent flap in the protection of our sleeping bags, to call it the sack race from hell would be an understatement. Outside, shivering in the cold night air, I immediately realize what's happened and re-entering the tent fumble for my torch to see land crabs scurrying around all over the floor. Hiding the shredded bin liner the crabs clawed their way out of in a side pocket in my Bergen I shout.

"It's OK lads, they're not scorpions, they're harmless land crabs!" When all three return, locate their torches and evict the 'scorpions' one by one we shake out our sleeping bags and settle down to sleep, then, just as were drifting off, with typical airborne relish one of the Jocks casually murmurs. "I never knew you could have crabs that big!"

Who can possibly sleep after such an apt comment.

* * *

Before moving to our next location we do two drops in daylight with heavy equipment containers. On the second drop I take out my Instamatic camera from inside my smock and get off a quick shot of the canopies beneath me. Hastily returning it I lower my container and land with no problems. It's a stupid thing to do but the picture came out rather well.

A few days later the totally unexpected happens when we're passing through a narrow canyon in a convoy of two trucks and a Land Drover and come to a rapid grinding halt when we hear the unmistakable sound of gunfire. Moments later the Sergeant Major appears behind the tailgate or our truck, his expression dire as he declares a 'No Duff'* situation, that the gunfire is directed at us and calmly but emphatically orders us to run for cover. In a matter of seconds the trucks empty as everyone dashes to the protection of huge boulders on one side of the canyon walls. Matters become even more hairy when he reappears carrying a dark green steel box of 7.62 ammunition which he opens and crashing his hand through its bright tinfoil seal moves from man to man liberally handing out handfuls of live rounds. Holding my useless Sterling SMG for which there is no 9ml ammunition, I watch the men rapidly load twenty rounds into their magazines and snap them into the underside socket of their SLR's before cocking them, aiming at the vast barren terrain but not shooting. With hardly a word of command a section of men goes on the offensive, covering each other in a movement technique known as 'pepper potting' as they move off to nearby gullies.

For the next hour or so, with the merciless sun beating down on us, there's no more firing and when the re-con guys return to the trucks and move on. Much later the Sergeant Major collects all the live ammo and will make no comment one way or the other the matter. So what happened, who the hell was shooting at us? Some of the men reckon maybe some disgruntled old hill farmer had taken at pop at us, others say it was more likely to be the SAS who were in the area training the Trucial Scouts and taking a few wide shots at us. We never found out, but what lingers in my memory of it is how normality can change in a split second to fearsome confrontation, how the training of what are mostly reservist soldiers instantly kicked in initiating an almost gleeful reaction to load rifles with live ammo and take on all comers. Whoever did it and for whatever reason, the first few moments when we ran toward those boulders were terrifyingly real. What lingers most of all is my reaction of murderous aggression and concern at whatever cost to myself for the men around me. A reaction as time served among soldiers as it is universal...

* In military jargon, when the words 'No Duff' are called out, as they can be at any time by any individual soldier, it literally means the situation, whatever it is, must be regarded as both threatening and real.

On the day ending six weeks of unforgettable mileage in the UAE the men I served with presented me with a tankard that decades later has pride of place in my home.

The picture came out rather well...

My Tankard

The guy who sells nail clippers...

The cooling bath at Wadi Shawkah

CHAPTER EIGHT

THE APOLOGY

Cardiff - 1956

At age ten my first experience of policeman was Constable Dobbs, a giant of a man with a moustache blacker than his shoulder cape who patrolled the streets of our council house estate on a bicycle. When I asked him if I could be a policeman when I grew up he replied.

"Only if you're a good boy and stay out of trouble, make your way home, your mams got cake!"

On the other hand he wouldn't think twice about raising boys onto tip toes with a good grip on their ear for a stern lecture if he thought they were knocking front doors and running away. Rather than being feared, he commanded immense respected. Our generation grew up with increasing respect by watching serials such as Dixon of Dock Green and Gideon of the Yard etc.

As time passed bringing a divorce, a second marriage and an overwhelming urge to be an author, apart from writing about other life experiences I could draw on six years of travel and unbelievable mileage wearing a red beret. By the 1980's I'm self-employed doing property maintenance and voluntary work for my local Victim Support Group. Late one night, following a call out from one of my customers, a distraught pensioner, I'm driving home in my Transit van, the streets are deserted except for a single policeman who seems to be having something of a confrontation with three youths. I immediately stop but continue when the youths go one way and the policeman the other. That policeman would never know he had a someone watching his back if things got ugly. My new wife Elly and I live in a block of flats, at eleven pm on a Sunday evening we're watching the end of a Movie called *'Ryan's Daughter'* when we hear a knock on the front door. I open it to see a young policeman who immediately asks two questions, what's my name, and did I take procession of a walking stick from a group of children. When I answer I don't know what on earth he's talking about, with no further questions he arrests and cautions both myself and Elly and asks permission to search our flat. When I readily agree, telling him we have absolutely nothing to hide, he speaks into a phone clipped onto his collar and moments later two more policemen appear who proceed to search the flat, and although looking for a walking stick are opening drawers. All three then take us downstairs to a police car where were driven to a nearby police station. Whereas Elly is taken to an office to be questioned I'm locked in cell where someone has fingered his name onto a wall with his own excreta. About half an hour later I'm taken to an office where the arresting officer presses down a switch on a tape-recording machine. Constantly repeating I know nothing about a walking stick, and has he asked other tenants in the building, he states the children are adamant they gave the walking stick to us. It's four am before we're finally released on police bail and get little sleep before work the next day. The following evening I go downstairs and knock my neighbour's door, her name is Elaine, she lives with her boyfriend Roger who is autistic, exceptionally timid and inoffensive and could easily pass for an eighteen-year-old Rock Hudson. When Elaine opens the door it the first thing I see leaning against the wall in her hallway is a walking stick with a large silver pummel. Elaine explains some children found it in a nearby park and assuming it belonged to the old man who lives in a ground floor flat where we live knocked his door but getting no answer left it with her. When I inform her both Elly and I were arrested in suspicion of stealing it she explains she didn't have the time to take the stick to the police station. Returning to our flat I ring the police station and speaking to the arresting officer explain what's happened and asked him to collect the stick. Sometime later he knocks our door carrying the walking stick but when I comment Elly and I are now exonerated and deserve an apology for wrongful arrest and the ordeal of the previous night to my amazement he very smugly replies. "The police do not apologise!" Even more amazing he adds he's now arrested Elaine's boyfriend who he's taking to the police station for questioning. Informing him the lad's harmless and wouldn't think of stealing anything, he merely shrugs and walks down the stairs. The next day, in the childlike way he talks, Roger is clearly upset when he tells me he was questioned for some time about how the walking stick came to be in his home but being incapable of anything less than the truth was then released. Due entirely to the barbaric way we've been treated I turn on my word processor and visualising every detail begin writing about the arrogance of the policeman, the disgusting police cell, and how having no police record whatsoever didn't warrant five minutes of the benefit of the doubt. Things change from the top, not from the bottom. Printing out my text and placing in an unsealed envelope I address it for the attention of the Chief Superintendent and hand it in at the police station. Despite Elly's trepidation, I'm not letting go. Barely do I arrive home from delivering the letter when the phone rings and a male voice asks if I'll come to the station to 'sort things out'. When the caller states he's a Sergeant I insist I will only discuss matters with the top man and refuse the request. Minutes later the phone rings again and a different male voice stating he's an Inspector makes the same request and receives the same response. The next evening, when I reverse my van onto the forecourt of the flat a police car driven by a female officer comes to a halt and asks if I will go with her to the police station to see the Superintendent. When I tell her I want to shower, change and wait until my wife comes home so we can both see him, she smiles and drives off. Entering the police station wearing a blazer, grey slacks, a white shirt and a tie dotted with blue and white para wings we pass through the reception area to a long corridor where there begins a gauntlet of several policemen lean out from office doors to stare at us, meeting every stare head on we enter the Chief Superintendent's office where a polite middle-aged man with the insignia of his rank on the shoulders of his shirt shakes our hands and gestures to two chairs in front of his desk, sitting opposite us he comments he's read my letter, adding it's descriptive and very well written. As our discussion progresses, and I tersely describe how my wife and I were arrested after only two questions, matters lighten up considerably when I add that if we had had a parrot in a cage the officer would have arrested that as well. Nodding and briefly smiling, he assures us officers coming straight from police training have yet to learn when not to use their powers of arrest. When he enquires exactly what it is we want, I answer that from a small boy I was brought up to respect the police and I demand respect in return. Vigorously nodding, he assures us the officer concerned will receive a verbal roasting and going to great lengths to apologise on his behalf the meeting comes to an amicable end when I feel obliged to comment that same officer wouldn't hesitate to confront a dozen hairy situations but needs to learn the difference between having power and having common sense. On that note we all walk to the reception desk. When we again shake hands prior to us leaving, I smile when I glance up the corridor to see at how many office doors are suddenly pulled closed...

Interesting footnote
A few weeks later, I run into a solicitor friend and after giving him a concise account of events with the police I'm dumfounded that although representing the law, rather than saying anything in the least constructive he cautions I will forever be a marked man. In the decades since then, I have rarely spoken to a police officer...

Don't miss out!

Visit the website below and you can sign up to receive emails whenever Barrie David publishes a new book. There's no charge and no obligation.

https://books2read.com/r/B-A-NCTG-CZOQC

BOOKS 2 READ

Connecting independent readers to independent writers.

Did you love *Journey to Prague and other Mileage*? Then you should read *Luke Blake's Screenplay*[1] by Barrie David aka Simon Titlark!

Luke Blake's Screenplay

Barrie David

Normality to abject terror... In the blink of an eye... [2]

Events inspiring this story came from reading screenplay format versions of John Steinbeck's - 'Of Mice And Men' and Harold Brighouse's - 'Hobson's Choice'

Prologue....

Currently retired and living in the Vale of Glamorgan with my wife Elly, plus our dog and our cat I enjoy writing stories drawn from amazing life experiences in various parts of the world. Set in contemporary Arizona this fictional story was inspired by a helicopter flight into the searing heat and mind-boggling terrain of the Grand Canyon for a relaxing picnic. All was well until our pilot advised his six British

---

1. https://books2read.com/u/4AAZKK
2. https://books2read.com/u/4AAZKK

passengers we could explore the area, the nearby Colorado River etc, but to keep an eye open for rattlesnakes. We all looked forward to lifting off.

With the essence of the story being how complete normality changes in the blink of an eye to abject terror I drew on a factual incident when I was a Paratrooper/Medic billeted in a tented camp in the UAE and picked up a football sized rock to bang in a loose tent peg to see a large scorpion crawl from beneath it and halt between my hands before I instinctively reversed the rock to give it a terminal headache. Those terrifying milliseconds of unexpected fear and revulsion are portrayed in the opening scenes and continue, mercilessly, for the entire second half.

Barrie David.

SYNOPSIS

Luke Blake's Screenplay

Pheonix – Arizona

Yesterday...

At age thirty-six Jeffrey Blake is a genius at stock market trading whose obsession for more wealth creates scathing contempt in his fifteen-year-old son Luke, a sensitive aspiring writer of screenplays. When Jeffrey's wife Elena persuades a belligerent Luke to go on a man-to-man vacation in an RV with the father he despises hostility reigns until an air clearing blowout at the Grand Canyon brings a fragile truce. Picking up a starving mongrel Luke names Beric they meet grizzled Vietnam Veteran and Campsite Owner Clem Hudson who tells Jeffrey about an isolated lake at the peak of a nearby mountain range. Seemingly the perfect place to further bond with Luke, Jeffrey ignores Clem's warning about the hazardous trail getting to the lake and how a dense fog rapidly descends. For two weeks camped beside the lake all is well until the vigilant Beric warns of a distant rattlesnake severely un-nerving Jeffrey although he shoots it with his Winchester. With the weather changing they hurriedly pack up and leave but when Jeffrey takes the wrong trail the dense fog Clem warned about obliterates their surrounding forcing them to halt for the night where daybreak begins a nightmarish ordeal of stark unrelenting terror.

Also by Barrie David

Memories of Mileage Past
Journey to Prague and other Mileage

About the Author

As a life long lover of reading books and writing, I am contendedly enjoying my retirement and live in South Wales in the Vale of Glamorgan with my wife Elly plus our dog and our cat.

I love passing on life experiences to others.